Family is for Life

By Mary Mansell

© Mary Mansell 2018

ISBN: 978-1-9164868-2-9
Caracal Publishing, United Kingdom

All Rights Reserved. No part of this publication may be reproduced, stored in a retrieval system, or transmitted in any form or by any means—for example, electronic, photocopy, recording—without the prior written permission of the publisher.

Unless otherwise stated, all Scriptural references are taken from The Holy Bible, New King James Version®. Copyright © 1982 Thomas Nelson, Inc. Used by permission. All rights reserved.

COVER PHOTO: UNSPLASH.COM/John-Mark Smith

Dedication

To my wonderful children and grandchildren: Nicola and Jason, Shantaya and Divna; Abigail and Jason, Sterling and Henry; Daniel and Kelly, Amazon, T-J and Poppy; Jonathan and Hannah, Isabel and Liliana

and to the memory of their amazing 100% father, Norman A. Mansell

"Hugs help"

Preface

These messages began as weekly letters to our married sons and daughters. You will notice that some messages are from both Norman and Mary: these were initiated by Norman, who was a real "Barnabas". I took on the project when he passed away a few months into it: this collection is chosen from our joint efforts over about two years.

Introduction

In a world that has begun to despise authority, scorn biblical traditions and tear apart the family, parents may need some encouragement! Here are messages to cheer you on in your battle to succeed as a godly family. You will also find some practical tips for all ages and various occasions.

This cannot be a comprehensive guide to every aspect of marriage and parenting (there are plenty of volumes and websites to that end) but here we humbly pass on some tidbits of wisdom that have proved helpful in "Manselldom".

Norman and I did not do everything right in raising our children (who does?), and what did turn out to be right was through God's grace alone! A huge debt is owed to our godly parents and Bible teachers over the years, and the least we can do is to pass on some of the benefits of their investment.

If this book helps you and your family live and shine for the Lord Jesus Christ it will be worthwhile. I hope you enjoy our letters.

January Beginnings - Week 1

United Front

Dear Family and Friends,

We need solid families, and in these days it will certainly take more effort -and more prayer- than ever in order to achieve them! It may help you to consider how the two qualities of consistency and reliability play their parts.

Canny, wheedling, opportunistic, observant, knowing- are some of the adjectives that could be applied to almost any child. So, if asking Mum (Mom) doesn't work, then approaching Dad at the appropriate moment (e.g. when Mum is out of earshot) might produce the desired answer! Or they could try asking for something when there are visitors, or Mum is on the 'phone and only half listening...

Children need to face a **united, consistent response** from both parents. We would point out that plentiful communication is vital to this end!
Parents, it would seem you have 3 possible answers to any request: (a) YES (possibly with qualification), (b) NO and (c) MAYBE....
Whatever your answer, **stick to your word**!

For example: You've agreed to take the children swimming at the pool... Alas, you arrive to find it closed for repairs or a Gala Event, but you make calls or ask Google and find a pool that is open and drive there. (Is an hour's driving reasonable in order to keep your word?)

Invaluable trust is built every time parents keep their word. Being reliable parents will actually make your job easier! Children **thrive on living within barriers** that don't crumble when challenged. They will test their boundaries, but *united* and *trusting* families stand!

Many blessings for the New Year, Norman and Mary.

January Beginnings - Week 2

Forgiveness

Dear Family & Friends,

Life as a child is simple, but has its limitations. If the parents are kind and loving (normal, that is), then food, warmth, clean laundry, and a comfy bed are always provided. If, on the other hand, (mercifully rare) the home is a disaster then what is a child supposed to do? Children of such disaster cannot change it and sooner or later may need to forgive much.

However, addressing normal parents, who willingly provide as well as they can for their children (which is NOT spoiling them), let me ask: How is the "emotional tone" in your home?

'Eat your vegetables', 'Comb your hair', 'Change those trousers', 'Elbows off the table' ... etc. may result in fine-looking, polite children, and that is fully commendable.

But is it balanced with phrases like: *'What are you drawing?', 'Give us a hug', 'We're so proud of you', 'Well done', 'You are my favourite 4-year-old)', 'Let me read you a story', 'We love you'* and **'We forgive you'**?

This is entitled *Forgiveness* because in the midst of busy

lives, **we must be sure to express forgiveness** to our little ones; it is so far-reaching. A hug, kiss or hair-ruffle will assure them that they are loved and secure. My recipe: 2 caresses for every correction.

Again, many blessings for the New Year!

See you next Friday, Norman and Mary.

January Beginnings - Week 3

Time

Dear Family and Friends,

How we spend our time this year may not always be our decision. Sleep will account for a good portion, work and routine activities for a further part but our priorities are reflected in how we use the spare hours.

Selflessly or selfishly? It is a decision.

Men, if you are a husband, your wife wants to have your undivided attention **frequently**. Arrange a "date", if necessary, to get away from distractions of T.V., 'phone, computer, sports etc, and just talk and listen (x2) to the one you promised to love and cherish.

Also, Men, if you are blessed with children around the home be sure to spend time with each of them regularly... daily should be the aim, plus an occasional outing with Dad alone. An ice cream cone at McDonald's currently costs less than £1.00 ($1.50).
Sure, you need time to yourself, but it just might have to be briefer and less frequent than you'd like; unchecked self interest will destroy relationships.

Ladies, for better or worse and even if you go out to work, the home is basically your domain. Nobody wants to come home to a mess! Train family members to help by all means, but clean clothes, food on the table etc. need your time and attention too.

Of course, one day each year (Mothering Sunday) you are thanked and regaled with treats... Alas, nest-building and maintenance are, like the rising sun, daily activities, essential but not always appreciated -but the sacrifices will be worthwhile!

We hope this helps. If you have friends who might benefit from a little avuncular (not sure what the female equivalent is) input, please pass this on.

See you next Friday, Norman and Mary.

January Beginnings - Week 4

Money

Dear Family and Friends,

"*MONEY....answers everything**," said Solomon, who knew a thing or two, and had plenty of this world's wealth but failed miserably in his family life.

This is too big a topic to cover comprehensively, so merely a few pointers are offered here.

My idea of a normal family is: Husband provides, wife spends judiciously and children lack for nothing. Of course, it could be argued that today "normal" means two incomes are required.

Be careful! Happiness and contentment are not obtained by possessions, but by relationship.

Husband, love your wife and display generosity towards her.

Wife, be content and live within the family budget.

Children, be grateful for your home and honour Mum and Dad.... it leads to a long life!

See you next Friday, Norman and Mary.

*Ecclesiastes 10:19 –New King James Version

January Beginnings - Week 5

Heaven is a wonderful place...

Dear Family and Friends,

On Monday I was speaking with my 4-year-old grandson on his birthday. He asked what I was going to do that day, so, not wanting to tell him I was about to attend a funeral, I said, 'I'm going to a special service.'

But he wanted to know more: 'What are you going to do at the special service?' So I replied, 'We are going to say goodbye to someone who has gone to heaven.' 'Oh', he said, 'I like heaven!'

Yes, if we have even a rough idea of the place where the Lord lives - where the angels and other beings worship continually, where there is awesome beauty and no sin, no sickness, no sorrow but everlasting, pure joy instead – we will like heaven too!

Saying farewell to someone who leaves this life for that one is still hard, since we were not built for this separation; but even a child can appreciate that God has opened wide the gates of **a wonderful home for us for us who believe in Jesus**.

And the Christian's great comfort is that we will see

each other again because Jesus Christ is Himself the Resurrection and the Life.

Do you look forward to heaven? Do your children know it is a real place where they will go one day, too? No-one will be disappointed in it; that is certain.

See you there, if not before!

Blessings to you all, Mary.

February Lifters - Week 6

Hearts

Dear Family and Friends,

Hearts, hearts everywhere! This is 'heart month' in more ways than one, it seems!

The Bible has a lot to say about our hearts. One command that Jesus reiterated was that we should **'Love the Lord our God with all our heart, soul, mind and strength'**. How can we love the Lord with all our heart?

One pastor has pointed out that the hero Samson, who was dedicated to God before he was born (even his hair was consecrated!) had a **divided heart**. His affections were divided.

Jesus said, 'If anyone loves Me he will keep My word'.

So, if we love Him with all our heart, it won't show up merely in singing sweet songs! Surely it must mean loving Him above anyone else, anything else, above our own ambitions, above our own life and keeping his commands? Help us, Lord!

You could **read about Samson* together as a family** and notice that, tragically and famously, he failed to centre his heart on God's will and so lost everything.

On the other hand, there is great reward in keeping Jesus' words!

When our hearts are totally given to Him we will be *doing* those words and living a successful life for Him.

Just imagine it! *Forgiving people, praying with faith, casting out demons, healing the sick, raising the dead, making disciples...*

Blessings to you all, Mary.

*Judges Chapters 13 to 16

February Lifters - Week 7

Treats

Dear Family and Friends,

Have you noticed how many things God included in Creation that we don't actually need? There are millions of expressions of His love for us; **He delights in just blessing us with treats.**

He designed roses, bougainvilleas, cocoa beans (for chocolate!), precious stones, music, views, robins, penguins, butterflies, miles of sand and waves.... the list is endless. Ask your children to come up with some favourites!

The Lord realised that Mankind was not made merely to work. We are not here only to study, commute and build or even only to worship! **He made us with a great capacity to enjoy the varieties in life.**

To Moses He laid out plans for annual holidays and feasting, and He ensured that beautiful and tasty things grew all over the Promised Land (Israel), as they still do today. Milk they needed; honey was an extra! Wheat and barley may have sustained life, but figs, grapes, dates and pomegranates certainly added to it!

In the Northern Hemisphere, it is presently a grey time of year; but even if you live in the sun somewhere else, this is still a good time to ensure that your family enjoys some of the planet's treats.

Just walk around looking for snowdrops, or put some marshmallows on the hot chocolate... collect funny pebbles on the beach or watch clownfish at the aquarium.

We were made for treats - they are so encouraging!

Blessings to you all, Mary.

February Lifters - Week 8

Friendship

Dear Family and Friends,

Whoops! This is a day late because we hosted a birthday party for a friend, and by the time ten of us had enjoyed Chinese take-away, trifle, birthday cake, chocolates and coffee with friendly banter as the presents were opened and cards read...it was very late.

This group of friends has met together several times a year for more than ten years. (Absent from the celebration were several of the regulars, including one travelling in Israel and another in Eire.)

Why is such friendship valuable? Because **we are not 'islands'!**

Every one of us needs other humans to relate to, to share our lives with. Some will claim that cats, dogs or horses – or even budgerigars!- come close to fulfilling their need for friendship, and that cannot be denied.

Even children recognise the joys of being respected and loved by a person who can keep their confidences, tell them the truth, learn their likes and dislikes and love them in spite of their faults.

Do your children have the friends they need? Do your best to facilitate godly friendships for them at every age.

We know the **best Friend is Jesus**: spend plenty of honest time with Him yourself and let your children know that he is the closest one!

Then cherish your God-given friendships, even from a distance, and please include in your family circle those who might otherwise be alone. Sowing friendship will always bring rewards.

See you next Friday, Norman & Mary.

February Lifters - Week 9

Love

Dear Family and Friends,

Everything that was created, was made in and by **Love** – including the rules by which to live! A wise parent or grandparent will introduce those principles within the daily context of the strongest and purest, most personal love. It has been said that **love** is the most powerful factor in education: who will not swiftly learn the first directions for life whilst sitting on Mum's or Dad's lap with loving arms around them and a picture book? Even in this cyber age, there is no substitute!

Teenagers may not appreciate learning in that way any more (!), but please remember that the original *laws* (I prefer the word '*Torah*,' meaning Godly direction) were given not with a pointing finger but from a smiling heart of tremendous **Love.**

See you next Friday, Mary
and Norman (recovering in hospital)

March Reflections - Week 10

Princes

Dear Family and Friends,

In Psalm 45, the bride is advised that her sons, or offspring, can become 'princes in the land' - I'm sure the sentiment works for princesses too.

We might feel to *pray and intercede* for our own children along this line, so what does it mean?

Everyone knows that a PRINCE will inherit the Kingdom and rule it. Therefore, as a child, he learns to appreciate his roots, to understand authority and the stewardship of time, talents and possessions. He is set apart, guarded, cherished and trained in government and warfare.

Because the world is watching, and because of his destiny, **a prince is a model**. He listens to godly counsel, embraces learning and does not abuse his body or mind. He honours his parents, is pure in heart, generous, compassionate and an advocate of the Kingdom.

He fears the Lord and hides His Word in his heart: he hates sin but loves what is good. He is rich but invents ways of raising the poor; he is noble, yet a servant to everyone he meets.

Wow! There is surely more - but who would not be rewarded by son (or daughter) like that?

Confess those qualities over your offspring in this way, for example:

"I declare that my son, Caleb, is a prince in the land: he is kind and generous and has a servant heart"

Or, *"I declare that my daughter, Kaylee, is a princess in the land: she honours her parents, hates sin and loves what is good"*.

Pray on, Parents!

See you next Friday, Norman (still in hospital), and Mary.

March Reflections - Week 11

Combat Stress

Dear Family and Friends,

Every family will experience times of stress, even extreme stress, whether due to heath issues, the arrival of a new baby, unemployment, moving house or whatever.

Positive stress too, as in preparing for an exciting holiday or a wedding, can even prove destructive to adults and children alike.

Here are a few tried and tested tips for when you may need them!

In times of stress:

- Treat each other gently, love a lot ('hugs help')

- Let some non-essential chores wait

- Ask for and accept help and prayers from the willing

- Look after yourselves well with food and warm baths

- Get as much sleep and rest as possible

- Pause often to imagine the love of God around you and holding you together- He is.

See you next Friday; Norman (still in hospital) and Mary.

March Reflections - Week 12

Heaven on Earth

Dear Family and Friends,

Too many homes could be described as the opposite of Heaven on Earth!

People who have glimpsed or experienced Heaven and have returned tell us that Heaven is the pattern for everything good on Earth.

So, we can confidently pray over our homes:
'Your will be done on earth (in my home) **as it is in Heaven.***'*

God designed Family to be a 'mini heaven'; a place where God lives, relationship is priority, Love is the beginning and end, where there is perfect order and unity, where no sin is tolerated and blessings - even miracles, are normal.

The blessings include peace of mind, health, joy, creativity, compassion and the centrality of worshiping Jesus.

Sounds so good!

Certainly, a home like Heaven is worth your investment.

Ask the Holy Spirit to increase His Presence in your home; He wants to help you!

Love, and maybe see you next Friday; Mary (sorry not Norman).

March Reflections - Week 13

Good Friday or Passover?

Dear Family and Friends,

Sometimes it happens that Good Friday and Passover Eve fall on the same day. Whether they do so or not, you and your family could find a way to celebrate the Old Testament picture of Salvation!

A very simple way, which we ourselves will follow, is to have a good meal - possibly with other folk invited - and begin it by lighting two candles and thanking the Lord for His plan to rescue us all from sin.

Then, in between courses, someone can read parts of the **Passover account in Exodus Chapter 12.**

Then, do as Jesus did at His last Passover meal with his disciples: break and eat crackers (unleavened bread or *Matzah*) and drink wine or juice in remembrance and thanksgiving for **Jesus, our Passover Lamb.**

There is plenty more that can be said or done, but even this token will be a precious experience and a great illustration for children. Do try it!

See you next Friday. Happy week end! Mary.

March Reflections - Week 14

Judas' Choice

Dear Family and Friends,

'and they counted out to him 30 pieces of silver.....'

The above phrase caught my attention this morning (reading Matthew, Chapters 26-28) and I invite you to join the scene in my imagination...

> *Hovering awkwardly in some Pharisee's office, Judas' eyes are fixed on the slowly mounting piles of coins.* As each piece is added, he sees, involuntarily, yet another scene from the past three years and dismisses it, hardening his heart......

Coin One: Judas remembers the Master he is betraying was always meeting people's needs, but he says to himself, *'All this is mine!'*

Coin Two: He remembers how Jesus fed multitudes but he shrugs off the miracles; *'I'll take myself to the best restaurant with this.'*

Coin Three: They walked many miles in close friendship together but, *'I'll be riding from now on!'*

Coin Four: He was one of the loved and chosen Twelve but, *'Well, He must have made a mistake and so did I!'*

Coin Five: He witnessed the Lord's brave confrontations with Religion but, *'He shouldn't have asked for trouble!'*

Coin Six: He was there when a grateful woman poured fragrance over Jesus' head but *'I tell you, it was nothing but a waste!'*

And so on................ until Judas grabs his blood-money and departs.

He is long gone, dead in disgrace.

By contrast, the One who lived selflessly, in total trust of His Father, shared everything He had and eventually 'poured out his soul unto death' for us (see Isaiah 53) is now **GLORIOUSLY ALIVE FOR EVER!**

Blessings to you all as we celebrate Jesus, Mary.

P.S. Perhaps your children could act out or illustrate this scene and other ones? M.

April Thoughts - Week 15

Grandpa's Money Tips

Dear Family and Friends,

Children and money: good habits can last a lifetime. A few pointers here may prove helpful in encouraging responsibility, stewardship and generosity in your children.

a) **Pocket money**, which will vary with age and family finances, should be given regularly, not as a reward for work done but as a gift. Help your child to **give** a portion (10% is traditional); **save** a portion and spend the rest wisely.

My dad, who was a bookkeeper (*incidentally the only word in the English language with 3 consecutive double letters*) put our money in a pay envelope and marked it clearly with the amount, the date and our name and placed it on the meal table between the salt and pepper shakers every Friday.

b) **Reward money** is received by agreement for doing regular chores or for such one-off activities as vacuuming the family car. Again, help your child to **give** a portion (10% is traditional); **save** a portion and spend the rest wisely.

c) **Gift money**, such as comes from kind grandparents

or doting aunts should be treated the same.

Of course, the child should always thank the donor, whether in the case of a, b or c!

On a practical note, parents, give the money in such a form as is easily divided; not for example, a £5 note or $5 bill but the same amount in coins.

See you next Friday, Norman and & Mary.

April Thoughts - Week 16

A Praying Mum (Mom)

Dear Family and Friends,

What do you want for your sons and daughters?

One of Israel's former kings, Josiah, came to the throne at 8 years of age and led a national revival at the age of 20. Writer Rachel Burchfield comments, *'Behind every move of God is a praying woman'*..... *Josiah's mother, Jedidah, was the key to his godly, thirty-one year reign'*.*

I do believe that if our children are to fulfil their destinies in this world we mothers need to pray for them just as persistently as we carried them in the womb. No giving up! No short cuts!

The best, greatest, most influential thing we can ever do for a child is to pray for him or her 'from the womb to the tomb'.

That may, at times, involve intercession as intense as giving birth to them in the first place! But is it worth the effort? A resounding 'yes' from Jedidah, Mary of Nazareth, Susannah Wesley and a few other notables!

So, I encourage all parents, but mums especially, to pray for your children: **pray over your children, lay**

hands on them, prophesy as you pray for them and pray God's promises over them daily, audibly, boldly and with faith in your heart!

We mothers are not here only to serve cups of tea (coffee, ice water –pick according to your continent) but to change nations with the gospel of the Lord Jesus Christ. And we shall see our children do just that!

Blessings to you all you pray-ers, Mary.

*Rachel Burchfield, from her letter *'Raising a Josiah Generation'*
New Spirit-Filled Life Bible for Women ©2007 Thomas Nelson. Inc.

April Thoughts - Week 17

Shepherds and Sheep

Dear Family and Friends,

Since our children are, in a sense, our disciples or 'sheep', then we need to be, like Jesus, 'good shepherds' to them!

In John Chapter 10, Jesus contrasts good shepherds, who own their sheep, with hired hands who only watch them for the money. He says **the good shepherds really care about their sheep; they know them well (they may even name them!); they protect them, and their sheep know their voice.**

Do you as a parent spend enough time with your children to know their likes, dreams and struggles? Do you really care about their school life, their friends, their spiritual growth?

Would you lay down your own plans in order to nourish your relationship with them, stand up for them, pray for them every day?

No doubt some children want to run and hide when they hear their parents' voice: how sad! Words of love and understanding, affection and tenderness will bring a better response! And in an atmosphere of compassion they will get to know your heart.

There are plenty of (rather soggy!) sheep in the UK, and I have watched shepherds trudging the fields to tend their ewes and rescue their lambs. The shepherd truly is a fitting example for us all.

Blessings to you all, Mary.

April Thoughts - Week 18

To Heal the Hurt

Dear Family and Friends,

There is a lot of pain in this world, and *'hurting people hurt people'*. I mention it for three reasons:

1. It usually explains *explains* why that shop assistant is so grouchy; why your child's teacher seems vindictive; why the next door neighbour yells at his kids and many more scenarios.

2. *Compassion*, rather than a negative reaction, could go a long way towards reversing the situation, and *forgiveness* even further.

3. Jesus came to heal the broken-hearted (the abused, the rejected, the bereaved, the victims.....) and the oppressors. **He wants to do that through us.**

One small boy*, on his mother's birthday, took a gift of flowers to the Communist guard who was holding both of his parents imprisoned for being pastors.

Who could your family reach out to, write a card to or smile at this week? It just might start to heal the hurt.

Blessings to you all, Mary.

*Mikhail, son of Richard and Sabrina Wurmbrand (Romania)

May Musings – Week 19

A Sense of Adventure

Dear Family and Friends,

Can you imagine that some folk in this day and age, and in the Western world, still live and die without travelling beyond their own county (state/province) or country?

Yet, what a wonderful planet we are given to explore and enjoy!

Children need to know from an early age that there is far more to experience than the nearest city or beach. We can stimulate them by various means to look further abroad and expect to be blessed with much **adventure** in their lives.

Here are some suggestions:

- Talk about other countries a lot, using souvenirs, flags, national dress, picture books and the internet

- Hang a world map on a wall near your meal table

- Invite people from far-away places to your home

- Rent, find on the internet or borrow adventure DVD's featuring expeditions, jungles, missionaries, the Antarctic and third world peoples etc.

- Start writing emails to a missionary family or some children in a third-world orphanage and put their photos up

- Plan a **minor family adventure** like a canoeing or camping trip within your country; then pray about and **plan an overseas adventure!**

Your children will grow up the richer, and will, hopefully, grasp this truth: that it is possible to live *anywhere* God calls them to be.

People who embrace God's way of life are **born for adventure!** Please note that David Livingstone, Mary Slessor, Hudson Taylor and Roland and Heidi Baker did not change nations by staying home!

See you soon - not next Friday: away on adventures until next month!   Love, Mary.

May Musings - Week 20

Signs of the Times

Dear Family and Friends,

God demonstrated His longing for a family when He chose an Iraqi named Abraham and promised him and his barren wife, Sarah, children as innumerable as the stars. He also promised to richly bless him and give him a land to call home.

Does God keep His promises?

There is one outstanding sign in the Earth today: one 3-D illustration that is visible to every nation and is fairly shouting, "Look! God is still in charge of the planet!" What is it?

It is **the existence of the State of Israel**, reborn in accordance with ancient prophecy on 14th May 1948. More than that, the tiny state has survived multiple hostilities and media haranguing to become a world leader in such areas as technology and modern agriculture.

But we are not concerned here with a geography lesson.

The point is that God's Word is true; in this prominent case it has already come to pass and therefore **what His Word says is yet to be** *will also happen!*

The Lord Jesus Christ will return to Jerusalem as He promised and, judging by the signs of the times, very soon.

Do make your family aware of the Sign that Israel is, and do *'pray for the Peace of Jerusalem'* and the Jewish people regularly.

We owe them huge debts for 'the blessings of Abraham', our Bible and our Saviour!

Blessings to you all, Mary.

May Musings - Week 21

Sparrows

Dear Family and Friends,

A tiny hatchling fell from its nest in our rooftop and hid in the garden for several days: the parent birds watched over it and fed it constantly until it was able to fly away.

Jesus said that in His day you could buy two sparrows for a penny (and make yourself some soup?), yet our Father sees and cares about whatever happens to one of them: *'do not fear therefore; you are of more value than many sparrows'.**

What a comfort to know that God is not only the Creator, not only the Governor of the whole universe, but also our **loving, compassionate Father!**

'His eye is on the sparrow........ '

He knows exactly where you are and where each of your children is at today.

Blessings to you all, Mary.

* Matthew 10:31 New King James Version

May Musings - Week 22

Let there be joy!

Dear Family and Friends,

Who was sorry when the Prodigal Son returned home? One child replied, 'The fatted calf!'

That is an old one, yes: but please note what accompanied the resulting feast: **music and dancing**!

Is there plenty of music in your house and even some dancing around the kitchen or lounge?

Children naturally create joy and thrive on joy; far be it from us to quench all of it! It is a feature of a home that is like 'Heaven on Earth' and brings a real balance to all the correction that must take place.

What makes you and your children laugh and jump for joy?

Blessed is the family that can have a good time laughing together around the table!

Joy doesn't have to be expensive: singing in the car or a simple picnic will suffice, but you could also invite the neighbours to a big BBQ and add some happy tunes!

Life too intense lately?

Invent a reason to turn on the music, eat treats and make merry with your friends. A prodigal might even join you.

Love, Mary.

June Sunshine - Week 23

Daddy

Dear Family and Friends,

All the children were clicked into their car seatbelts one Sunday morning recently and the family was merrily on its way to church when the littlest girl burst into tears.

She sobbed in anguish from the back seat, 'Daddy! Daddy! I forgot my dolly!'

What would you have done?

I watched this daddy pull over, turn the car around and drive back to the house to search for that doll and bring it to his grateful daughter.

Is that being 'soft'? No, it's being compassionate. It's being like our Father God who 'is full of compassion and gracious'.

Like the Lord Jesus, a human father can also be strong in the face of disobedience or injustice, but if he balances his love of truth with his love of mercy he will be a grand model of 'the Father of mercies' to his family.

Blessings and grace to all daddies!

See you next Friday.   Love, Mary.

June Sunshine - Week 24

Four A's

Dear Family & Friends,

No doubt all you fathers are annually inspired (and, hopefully, honoured) on Father's Day.

Here in Swindon we are considering being **parents after God's pattern**. The following condensed points may be good tips for you too – they are reproduced with thanks to Pastor Giles Stevens, who is raising a young family.

1) AFFECTION
It is important to **verbalise our love** for our children, to look them in the eyes and actually say, 'I really love you!'

2) ACCEPTANCE
Children should know they are **loved because they are precious** to us, not on the basis of their looks or their achievements!

3) ATTENTION
A good parent cares about their child's life enough to be **interested in the details** (e.g. of their day, their friends n their concerns)

4) AUTHORITY
'Discipline makes disciples', but beware that it is carried out in gentleness, humility and patience - **not anger**!

The Lord will surely help us with all the above because it is clearly how He treats us!

See you next Friday.   Love, Mary.

June Sunshine - Week 25

Here Comes the Groom

Dear Family and Friends,

Walking in a sunny, country setting last Saturday, my friend and I (plus her little dog) happened upon six soldiers in their best uniforms, waiting outside a church porch and brandishing swords. The bells were pealing, causing the dog to howl in chorus, and various folk had their cameras at the ready, so, of course, we stood there until the bride and groom emerged to their guard of honour.

A flock of bridesmaids and gorgeously dressed guests followed them into the fresh air and all threw petals on cue as the families rejoiced and the moments were recorded.

There is something very gripping about a wedding! How many millions around the world will watch a British Royal Wedding?

Today I see in John Chapter Three that Jesus' cousin, John, the most prophetic person of his day, saw himself as the Best Man and **Jesus as the Bridegroom** for whom he has waited, the One he recognises with great joy.

Folks, **the Lord Jesus Christ is coming back for His bride**. We are that glorious Bride! How joyful will that wedding be?

Jesus really is returning to Earth to reign and He will, one day soon, stage the most awesome wedding feast imaginable.

Blessings to you all, Mary.

June Sunshine - Week 26

Desperate

Dear Family and Friends,

Yesterday I heard about the prayer life of a toddler who lives, as does her entire family, in a nation under real and constant threat from its hostile neighbours.

She does not sweetly fold her hands and lisp, '*Now I lay me* ...'! **No, this little girl lies face-down on the floor and cries out to the Lord!**

What does this tell me? She is not mature enough to have seen this modelled in Scripture or to have decided it is the most appropriate manner in which to speak to Almighty God: **she is copying the way her mother prays in the home.**

There is desperation in the heart of her parents and grandparents. It amounts to, '*O Lord, we need You! We desperately need Your help, Your protection for ourselves and for our nation. We desperately need You in our lives....*'

In its opening lines, Psalm 42 paints a picture of real thirst: a deer in a hot, dry land is searching for a brook, panting for a drink of water. The song-writer compares that image to his own thirst for God: '***My souls pants for You... yes, thirsts for the living God***'.

How desperate are we for the Lord? For His presence, His power, His comfort, His refreshing?

Are we desperate to receive from Him the anointing, revelation, courage, words of direction, miracles and all else that we need....?

A reality 'litmus test' will reveal either children praying trite recitations or **children who are real with God and thirsty for Him.**

Blessings to you all, Mary.

July Ideas - Week 27

Sit long, Talk Much

Dear Family and Friends,

'What is this life if, full of care, we have no time to stand and stare?*.... Or sit and talk!

Do you have family members with whom you have not held a conversation since the last wedding or graduation? And after a funeral, do the mourners usually say, "We must get together on a happier occasion"...?

Good idea!

Even the telephone and social media are no real substitute for a long, face-to face catch-up over food with cousins, siblings or, perhaps, your own children.

Who can put a value on the hugs exchanged between parents and adult offspring returned from years in a foreign country, months in the Big City or a tour of duty? How priceless are the subsequent hours of sharing to and fro!

So, start now, even with small children, to relax as much as you can and just converse and laugh!

- Stop the car to watch deer, pat horses, stare at a view

- Sit together as long as you dare in the park or the restaurant (with your phone put away!)

- Lie on your backs around a campfire and pick out planets

- Ask Grandma to tell you her stories one more time

On a rustic plaque in rural, laid back Nova Scotia I noticed the above inscription: *'Sit long, Talk much'*. The family life in that Canadian province is famously strong.

See you next Friday, Mary.

*William Henry Davies, *'Leisure'*, 1911

July Ideas - Week 28

Promises

Dear Family and Friends,

Where would we be if God changed his mind about the universe every day? If the sun did not always rise, the tides were not controlled and the rules of physics went haywire because the Lord withdrew the rules set by His own words, we could not survive!

Our daily security on this planet exists only because **our Creator keeps to His word.**

With precious little trust left in this world, parents need to build all the faith they can into today's children. If we can teach them to trust God's promises, they will have a secure foundation for life's vicissitudes - the unchanging love of Father God.

So, since our children learn the character of God by looking to us (or should do!), I urge all parents to be consistent and trustworthy. If you make a promise, **do your utmost to keep that promise** (or don't make it)!

That party, even if it rains; that costume, even if you have to sew all night; that day fishing trip, even if the boss has offered you double pay; that puppy, even if the price goes up... the possibilities are endless.

If we keep our promises to our children (negative ones too) we build in them a trust that will be of incalculable worth in the future.

See you next Friday.   Love, Mary.

July Ideas - Week 29

Rest

Dear Family and Friends,

Rest, holiday, time off! Chill out, relax... we all need it. The Creator is wise and he stipulated that only six days out of every seven were for work!

As English children wend their way home on the final day of school here (at last!), millions of parents, bus drivers and teachers may be looking forward to sleeping in next week - and having no lunch boxes to fill!

Time to refresh brains, bodies, emotions and spirits.

Suggestions as follows:

For the brains - play some simple family games and let the little ones win.

For the bodies - swim (in the sea if possible), lie on a beach, snooze in a hammock ... with no guilt!

For the emotions - take a picnic/ BBQ to your favourite lake, riverside or hilltop and meditate on the view.

For the spirit - read a Psalm together aloud each

morning. Try these for a start: 145, 16, 1 and 103.

Happy summer!

Blessings to you all, Mary.

July Ideas - Week 30

Differences

Dear Family and Friends,

You know, it is possible to use a 'blanket approach' for all the children in your nuclear family. Not wise!

For example, take planning a week-end camp in the woods by a lake.

Dad can hardly wait; son aged 9 pictures himself with hatchet and matches sorting out the camp fire, whilst Mum faces a massive packing job for every eventuality, and soon-to-be-teenage daughters shudder at the very thought of tents.

Time to respect differences!

How about Dad and son going camping overnight while Mum and daughters have a quiet evening at home with their favourite 'phone-in food, maybe a movie that they enjoy and a shopping trip the following day?

Yes, we do many things together as a family... meals, visiting Aunty Dolly, church, outings and holidays, but we need to acknowledge and make room for the differences in our family members.

One size does not fit all!

Getting the balance right without catering to "foibles" would tax even Solomon, but nobody ever said raising a family was easy!

See you next Friday, Norman & Mary.

July Ideas - Week 31

Old-fashioned?

Dear Family and Friends,

Not everything *'New'* and *'Latest'* is necessarily the best!

Quality is often advertised as *'Traditional'*, as in *Traditional Roast Dinner* or *Traditional Farmhouse Accommodation*.

How about old-fashioned or traditional **good manners?**

It does take effort and example, but training our children in such customs as deference to their elders, authorities and the infirm will certainly confront today's trends in selfishness.

Even a boy of 6 can open a door for a lady (if she accepts his help), and a 3-year-old can phone or scribble her thanks to Auntie!

What a delight it was, a few days ago, to observe a grown young man hold his plate of chocolate cake until Grandma was seated, and then thank her profusely before eating it! That politeness was instilled early and should take him far.

Plain gratitude and respect are old-fashioned, yes, but they are qualities that help build the self-less character of Jesus in all of us.

Come on, you can set the fashion in manners!

Blessings to you all, Mary.

August Chats - Week 32

Jonah

Dear Family and Friends,

Here is a suggestion for this week: sit down with your whole family and read the **dramatic, true story of Jonah** all the way through. It has only 4 short chapters but quite a few lessons! (Plenty of songs and illustrations exist to enliven your experience.)

What can you, or even your small children, notice about the following:

The consequences of Jonah's disobedience? (Chapter 1)

How he got back on track? (Chapter 2)

God's mercy to him and then to an entire city? (Chapter 3)

One particular sentence from Jonah's prayer out of the depths comes as a re-assurance that we are serving the right God, the only Living God who can forgive and offer a second chance.

It reads, *'Those who cling to worthless idols forfeit the grace that could be theirs'.*

Jonah clung to the right God. He had a second chance, and he must have been outstandingly thankful for Amazing Grace!

Blessings to you all, Mary.

August Chats - Week 33

Great Expectations

Dear Family and Friends,

Every one of us was **born with a specific plan** already detailed in our Heavenly Father's mind. And that means that every one of us has a wonderful purpose to fulfil!

Can we help our children and grandchildren to pursue great expectations in their lives, higher dreams than we ourselves cherished? Here are some suggested ways:

- Repeat over and over, in natural conversations, that **God has an awesome and exciting life planned for them.**

- Talk about their **dreams** with them and continually say, *You can do it! You can become that! You can go there!*

- In your own heart, **expect** your children to succeed, expect them to be happy, expect them to have adventures, expect them to choose God's best!

- Above all, **pray** and prophesy over them that every purpose for their being here on earth in this generation will be fulfilled.

If we defend and nourish such expectations, they will surely come to pass and bring much joy to the whole family!

And all the glory goes to Father God.

Blessings to you all, Mary.

August Chats - Week 34

Treasured Words

Dear Family and Friends,

In the course of turning out a house recently, we came across manuals for various appliances, most of them untouched. It seems no-one had needed detailed instructions for fitting a vacuum bag or re-installing the electric cooker (stove).

But in every room we found well-loved or even worn out versions of the one and only 100% reliable manual for life: **Bibles** of every kind.

The owners of those particular books had consulted them every single day over many decades; inside they had found *their Maker's directions* for every possible aspect of life and learned to rely on His advice above that of amateurs like themselves.

It still is by following the Manual that families discover how to trust God, how to faithfully support one-another in good times or tough times, how to enjoy life, how to raise their children, how to pray, what to do with their money, what their future in Heaven is like, and a host of other vital subjects.

Folks, do open the pages of God's Word every day;

relish the rich contents and you (like my parents) will not be sorry, but successful!

Jesus lived off God's words, and we too need them more than food. Be humble enough to follow the Maker's Manual and point your children to it for a truly amazing life!

That is guaranteed.

Blessings to you all, Mary.

August Chats - Week 35

Boundaries

Dear Family and Friends,

'Stay away from the edge!', 'Come down!', 'Don't go past the blue floats!'

We consistently set boundaries and limits for our small children - for their protection, of course. Some little ones will readily comply, whereas others will try our patience unto exhaustion!

However, if we persist in re-enforcing the limits we have set, many life-lessons will be learnt and many trips to the Emergency Ward (Room) may be avoided!

How about our own, not-so-simple limits? Do our children observe parents who constantly work seven days a week, or perhaps, spend money they haven't got, or watch TV until dawn?

If, on the other hand, they see us obeying authorities and practising self-control, guess what! That could actually 'rub off' "!

The 8-year-old just might switch off that game to get his homework done, and the 17-year-old might bring your car back intact on the dot of 10.00 pm.

Amazing!

So don't be afraid to set many boundaries for your family or to uphold them.

Our loving Father God set plenty of limits for us and they are not given to 'spoil our fun' but for our protection: **He, too, longs to see us all both safe and successful.**

Blessings to you all, Mary.

September Seasoning - Week 36

Schooldays

Dear Family and Friends,

The old adage says 'Schooldays are the best days of your life' and some folks would agree- yes, they should be filled with fun, friends and discoveries.

How can you help your youngsters through these days that that can also be threatening and demanding?

Plenty of practical tips exist; here is one of my favourites:

> Write **brief encouragements** in marker pen on lunch bags (sacks), or put notes inside lunch boxes, e.g. 'Enjoy Swimming' or 'Happy Thursday' (just make sure it *is* Thursday- I never did live that one down!)

But I reckon the best thing of all for our family was the daily announcement, **'On the Mat!'**

This meant it was time to gather inside the front door with everything ready for 'take off', and **Mum would pray over all those on their way to school.**

If you think about it, that makes for such security, such affirmation, such an invitation to Father God for His presence and protection!

You could do something similar at the breakfast table or in the car.

Do you know, the grown up offspring still come home and ask for the prayers *On the Mat* sometimes.

Happy schooldays!

Blessings to you all, Mary.

September Seasoning - Week 37

Heroes

Dear Family and Friends,

According to one translation, King David said, 'I will make the godly of the land my heroes'.*

Who are the heroes in your household?

Are they just rich, famous and celebrated, but their personal lives are blatantly ungodly, selfish and even violent? Or, are your heroes celebrated for noble reasons, whether they are rich or poor?

It is said that we become what we look at: so it would be good to be aware of those whom your children admire and it would also be good for you to to exercise guidance!

I recommend supplying your young readers with biographies of God's heroes and finding biblical cartoon films about them for the pre-schoolers. There are plenty of good ones on Netflix that you will enjoy too. (Animations are so clever these days!)

The highest example for both parents and children is, of course, Jesus Himself. Could you admire Him instead of some of the so-called heroes of our time?

You will not regret making Him your household hero!

See you next Friday, Mary.

*Psalm 101:6 - The Living Bible copyright © 1971 by Tyndale House Foundation. Used by permission of Tyndale House Publishers Inc., Carol Stream, Illinois 60188. All rights reserved.

September Seasoning - Week 38

Plenty, Plenty

Dear Family & Friends,

Here in UK we are still harvesting apples, tomatoes and various vegetables. Time to think about the 'God of Abundance' and all He gave to our planet!

He very obviously planned for His family of humans to live in **plenty**, not poverty. Something called **'poverty mentality'** is a leftover, **religious misconception.** Every family needs to guard against it as much as we guard against materialism!

Some people manage on very little income but you would never guess it from their contented conversation or their generosity: others may enjoy a greater income but constantly complain that they cannot afford this or that!

Here are some **tips** for nourishing biblical contentment and prosperity in your home:

- Deliberately **cut out** the phrase *'we can't afford...'* and change it to *'we are choosing to spend our money in a different way'*.

- **Practise being thankful**, extremely thankful, for

every good thing that comes to you.

- Never allow children to say, '*I want a...*', but train them to **pray with you about their needs and desires.**

Remember that our Heavenly Father is fabulously wealthy; as His children, we have access to His abundance.

Plenty - and plenty to give away!

Blessings to you all, Mary.

September Seasoning - Week 39

Pride and Practicality

Dear Family and Friends,

Mums (Moms), unless you are a Marines-trained, iron-pumping super-momma, there are going to be some times when you need help.

It is no shame to accept or even ask for help!

When your 6-year-old's birthday falls on the first day of the school year for himself and three siblings, let somebody else make the chocolate cake!

When you bring home a new baby to a houseful of toddlers and your mother-in-law is due to arrive, receive all the cleaning and cooking and laundry aid you can get!

And if that is not you, think about folk in your church or community who may not have the nerve to ask for help but are struggling to mow the grass, clean their windows or find a baby-sitter. Please have the courage to offer your energies or those of your bigger children!

Christianity is intensely practical, and our children need to see this. **'Love one another' needs muscles as well as smiles** and could turn you into a life-saver.

Blessings to you all, Mary.

October Colour - Week 40

Angels and Other Beings

Dear Family and Friends,

The **spirit world is real**, and sometimes children are more sensitive to the presence of generally unseen spiritual beings than we adults are. How can we help them to relate to those beings properly?

Simply put, it depends on where that being comes from.

Does it cause, for example, fear, nightmares or distress? Then it comes from the kingdom of **Darkness** and we can teach even a small child to **resist it** by saying aloud, "Go away in Jesus' name!"

From the kingdom of **Light** come angels of various sorts and we can expect their help at any time.

Children need to know that **God's angels** are not fairies, and have nothing to do with magic. They are not to be feared because they are strong, holy personalities sent from Heaven, well described in the Bible.

Encourage your children to **ask the Lord** for angels to protect them but not to worship them or pray to them!

All believing families can resist dark spirits; conversely, we can enjoy the ministry of angels.

We certainly do so already, much more than we realise!

Blessings to you all, Mary.

October Colour - Week 41

Banquet

Dear Family and Friends,

I have been watching the first DVD of a series about Windsor called 'The Queen's Castle'*. How fascinating to observe the lengthy and detailed planning for a state banquet!

The heights of splendour and the most sumptuous meal are being prepared for scores of guests seated at the gigantic, polished table set with gold-plated dishes and decorated with glorious flower arrangements. Only King Solomon 'in all his glory' fared as well!

Surely, we on earth are following the pattern of Heaven: these ideas come from our Creator who also loves beauty, order and majesty and He put the same desire for such in our hearts.

As we in our homes do our best to bless family and friends with beauty, food and gifts on special occasions, **think about Heaven** a bit!

It is so glorious, but the Lord Jesus left behind all that splendour and laid down His royal rights in order to identify with us in our need and give His priceless life for us.
And imagine, just for believing in Him, we are invited

to **the most awesome feast of all!**

At that banquet, called "The marriage supper of the Lamb" in Revelation Chapter 19, worship will be first on the menu, just as it is first here every day.

Blessings to you all, Mary.

The Queen's Castle, Matt Reid, RDF Media and HTI ©2005 Universal Studios

October Colour - Week 42

A Time to Honour

Dear Family and Friends,

Do you know what the 5th Commandment says? The Apostle Paul points out that it has a promise attached:

'Honour your father and mother ...that it may be well with you and you may live long on the earth.' *

The honouring of all authorities is going to begin in your home. So, Mum and Dad, you will reap honour if you sow honour!

Do speak politely to each other at all times (not just in public) and insist that children do the same - both to each other and to you, the parents, and all authority figures; in fact, to all people!

Honouring is not just for the lips, it must encompass obedience too.

Children need to see us adults keeping to the speed limits, crossing the road on the green light at a zebra crossing (crosswalk) and respecting doctors, teachers, police officers and the government etc.

It may be thought 'outmoded' to address someone as

Sir or Madam these days, or to serve someone ahead of yourself, but as we practise giving honour we will be more conformed to the nature of the Lord Jesus Christ, who really humbled himself.

I remember watching an older lady who was in the queue (line) for 'ladies first' at a large buffet dinner gathering. She filled a plate and then brought it to her husband to honour him! I was not the only shocked, modern wife who admired her humility that day.

Our marriages will be blessed, and our homes will definitely be more peaceful as we respect one another!

Could you surprise somebody with some *honour* today?

Blessings to you all, Mary.

*Ephesians 6:2-3

October Colour - Week 43

Impossible

Dear Family and Friends,

Someone has said that Christians are not called to do *great* things.... we are called to do *impossible* things!

People who have little or no faith in God can certainly do great things: people who believe in the Lord Jesus Christ need to be His imitators and **expect supernatural help to do** *impossible* **things.**

What is it that your family deems impossible? Is it owning your own home, taking an overseas holiday or repaying a debt?

Or is it, perhaps, something that appears impossible in another area – relationships to be restored, healing to come, loved ones to open their lives to the Lord, your marriage to be amazing?

Jesus demonstrated this truth: ***Nothing is Impossible with God!***

It only takes a little faith in a big God to ask for something that you know He wants to happen.

Let me encourage you to **believe again, pray and**

expect again! Adults and children alike will be dancing for joy.

Blessings to you all, Mary.

November Warmth - Week 44

Inside Story

Dear Family and Friends,

Today's message is basically for mums-at-home (*been there, done that*). **Do you ever feel like a prisoner** -same walls, same routine, same view and no travels?

Don't despair! You know, the Apostle Paul spent plenty of time in jail!

Once, he called himself 'the prisoner of the Lord'. I believe this is because he was confined, constrained in that place **according to the will of God**! After all, the Lord had chosen to break him out of prison before, but not this time! Therefore, some of his most productive ministry, his legacy letters, were prepared in that circumstance.

Mum-at-home, you are not really a prisoner; you are a **privileged person**, a chosen woman who is being moulded into the image of Jesus and exemplifying Him to precious little ones.

You are learning things that maybe university and career did not teach. Things like servanthood, compassion, longsuffering and patience (Ouch!).

Two tips:

- *Maintain joy.* Sing at the sink, laugh at little things

- *Maintain communications.* Speak to the Lord and to some other mum (mom) every day.

So, be in peace; all too soon your 'freedom' will be here again.

[Dads and those on the outside, give the lady an encouraging phone call today!]

Blessings to you all, Mary.

November Warmth - Week 45

Strength Comes!

Dear Family and Friends,

Guh-Bang! We were on a mission trip in Siberia and singing our way up the Ob River on a large *raketa* when the boat's drive shaft broke.

Stranded two hours from anywhere, the far-off bank barely in sight and without phones, the Russian lady who was both owner and captain must have been pretty glad of our prayers!

Our Ukrainian team-mates continued to worship in glorious harmony. I will never forget their rich voices and radiant faces!

Before too long a huge, cargo *raketa* loaded with timber slowed near us and, after some discussion, this is what happened: the strong vessel drew as near as possible and we were actually bound to it and then carried safely all the way to our destination by its engines.

When we run out of strength, when we cannot go forward by ourselves, **the Holy Spirit comes alongside us** and gives us His comfort and power.

He loves to do that. Mums and Dads, invite Him!

Blessings to you all, Mary.

November Warmth - Week 46

Feed Them

Dear Family and Friends,

When you brought your new baby home did you leave her to fend for herself, waiting for food and blankets to drop by? Of course not! Yet, sadly, many parents do not nurture their precious children spiritually!

Spiritual growth won't "just happen": it is our God-given responsibility, and most rewarding.

It is unlikely that today's little ones will receive biblical truth from either state school or television. **We are the ones who need to feed them** continually, daily making use of every opportunity to speak about the Father, the Saviour and the Holy Spirit.

It is not hard to cultivate knowledge of God, our Father and Creator as we enjoy His creation! It is equally easy to introduce Jesus, the Saviour from our sins, the Healer and the King, in our conversations and in teaching children to pray.

One mother I know encourages her children, even at pre-school age, to stop and listen to the Holy Spirit. She has been amazed at the appropriate, simple things they have heard from Him!

I truly recommend spending time in Bible picture books, even with babies and toddlers, always pointing out how wonderful Jesus is and how much we love him.

And do pray with them, without fail, at bedtime and at other times, getting the youngest to copy your words in prayer. Primary-school-aged children can enjoy reading with you, for example, **Luke Chapters 1 and 2 for the truth about Christmas!**

Older children, who are developing further spiritually, will bring you their own insights, and they need plenty of relaxed time after dinner (supper), or maybe beside you in the passenger seat, to discuss them with you. What a joy!

Blessings to you all; Mary.

November Warmth - Week 47

Hugs Help

Dear Family and Friends,

We all know that a new-born baby has many simple needs: food, warmth, dry nappies (diapers) and COMFORT. A child without this last need met may, tragically, 'fail to thrive'.

In fact, we all need plenty of comfort at every stage of life, don't we? It can be a harsh world!

So hug your children a lot, even when they are grown. Reassure them in times of fear, after correction or disappointment with wonderful, love-filled, squeezy hugs!

If you travel or move, make sure they can bring favourite soft toys. Even some elderly grandparents find immense comfort in hugging a plush puppy or cat.

Of course, if you are lost in the forests of Canada, the advice is: 'hug a tree!' Amazingly, it is a comfort, and it makes you stay in place to get found!

Our **unfailing comfort** is found in the love of the Lord Jesus Christ. Nothing is better than a hug from Heaven!

We can share plenty of that around in unashamed family hugging. It is one way to thrive!

Blessings to you all, Mary.

December Delights - Week 48

Quality Parents

Dear Family and Friends,

What if you lived in Israel around 5 BC and your name was Joseph or Mary - *the* Joseph and Mary?

And what if *you* too have been chosen, in this 21st Century, to raise precious children to fulfil their God-given destinies?

Let's see if you can check off qualities similar to those which the Lord regarded in Jesus' parents:

    God-fearing
    Knowing the Scriptures
    Sensitive to the Holy Spirit
    Obedient
    Courageous
    Full of faith
    Selfless
    Protective
    Energetic
    Trustworthy

What a tall order!

In Matthew Chapters 2 and 3, you can read the famous

story of those outstanding parents, and notice how **they made their biggest decisions based upon revelation from God,** not feelings, pressure of circumstances or head knowledge!

Now, be encouraged in your task; even if you didn't score well, the Lord Jesus is able to generate all those qualities in you and make you first-rate parents too!

Blessings to you all, Mary.

Delights - Week 49

Right Time

Dear Family and Friends,

Yochanan was an only child: his parents had actually given up hope of ever having a baby. But they had not lost their faith! True to their heritage, they persisted in serving the Lord and in supporting each other.

Then, at last and against all odds, it happened! Elderly Father got his prayers answered; elderly Mother conceived; another miracle on was on its way.

Not their timing, but **God's perfect timing** was in action, arranging all the jig-saw pieces for His redemption-plan to be enacted upon Earth.

Earlier this week, I had the joy of watching a beautiful, Primary School re-enactment of the next stage in God's great plan. Smile and imagine it!

Doesn't every Nativity Play fill us with awe? We wave at the kiddies, wipe our eyes and wonder again at the way the Lord came.

All the pieces were put in place by the God's wisdom: the prophecies, the Romans, the young couple, Gabriel, the star, the wise men, the census, the shepherds, the angels..........

And also the boy who grew up to be Yochanan (John) the Baptiser; **born at just the right time, to the right parents,** to become the greatest prophet of all.

Blessings to you all, Mary.

December Delights - Week 50

We Traverse Afar

Dear Family and Friends,

Happy Christmas!

A group of Eastern colleagues features in Matthew's account of the birth of Jesus. We call them *The Wise Men* and we add many speculations to what little we know of them from the Gospels.

For example, how many of them were there? And did they ride camels?

Anyway, what was so wise about their making an expensive and hazardous journey, across who knows how many lands, in first-century conditions? It was an undertaking fired only by their conclusions about a weird, bright star in the sky!

In the course of their journey they might well have become known as *The Crazy Men,* ridiculed rather like Noah was for his persistence in following directions from God.

But *'the proof of the pudding is in the eating'* and their

conviction paid off: they did find the new King and they did go down in history as the first Gentile worshippers of Emmanuel -God with us in the flesh.

The Bible says **'they rejoiced with exceedingly great joy'**: that sounds like jumping up and down, shouting, laughing and dancing, doesn't it?

Wise people find Jesus and find the real party.

Blessings and many joys to you all in this wonderful season! Mary.

December Delights - Week 51

Agape

Dear Family and Friends,

So – as Christmas comes and goes, what a good time to consider how your family is doing in the area of loving!

It is quite the challenge for parents, or anyone, to love in the way that God loves us! It seems that human beings, generally, can quite easily love those who love us, those who please us, those who meet our expectations and those who agree with us. We can even love strangers and unresponsive people to some extent.

But what about those (who may be our own children) who disobey, under-achieve, argue or are disrespectful at times? Do we, or should we, then withdraw our love from them?

God loved us and sent us his Best when we did not love or obey Him, and He still does - **not because we are good** but because He is made of the kind of love that attaches no conditions, **'agape love'**. He just loves because He is a lover.

Of course, God's kind of love includes discipline for us and for our families when necessary, but even then, **unconditional love** prevails to bring about change and restore relationship. It is so powerful!

We see 'agape love' in the real Christmas: Jesus leaving Heaven, being born on Earth for us and going on to provide forgiveness for us on the Cross.

Now that He lives in us, we actually have the same loving, forgiving resource to draw upon.

Please assure your spouse and your children that you will always love them unconditionally; that is, *whatever!*

Because love is for life, not just for Christmas.

Blessings to you all; Mary.

December Delights - Week 52

New Years' Eve

Dear Family and Friends,

Whilst youngsters in this country like to go up to London and blow whistles with the celebrating crowds, I must say I prefer to sit and **contemplate** in front of a glowing fire!

But after that, I shall stir my bones to go eat and have fun with my church as we prepare to praise and worship God during the first minutes of next year. There is something special about giving back to the Lord the **first** of what He has given to us: something that honours Him and blesses us.

As for the contemplation, we don't have to become monks to benefit from a little break from rushing about, working, watching T.V., playing games etc.!

Yes, your whole family could stop, maybe around candles on the coffee table, and pool their answers to a few pertinent questions, such as:

- **What is your favourite memory from the past year?**
- **What was your biggest surprise during the**

year?

- How many answers to prayer can you count?

Do add your own questions!

And then, turning to the year ahead, you could pray for each individual regarding their expectations and dreams.

Eat and drink special treats or share Communion....

Blow whistles if you have to!

Just be sure to meet the coming year with a strong assurance that God is in charge of everything and is holding us in His strong and loving arms. He has amazing plans to bless us all!

Happy New Year!

In Jesus' love, Mary.

MY FAMILY

Name   Birthday

SPECIAL FAMILY MEMORIES

Date   Occasion

MY FAMILY ADVENTURES

Date   Place

_____

_____

_____

_____

_____

_____

_____

_____

_____

_____

_____

_____

MY FAMILY GOALS

This year

_____
_____
_____
_____
_____

For the Future

_____
_____
_____
_____
_____
_____
_____
_____

MY FAMILY'S ANSWERS TO PRAYER

Request   Date of Answer

_____

_____

_____

_____

_____

_____

_____

_____

_____

_____

_____

_____

_____

_____

_____

www.ingramcontent.com/pod-product-compliance
Lightning Source LLC
Chambersburg PA
CBHW070954080526
44587CB00015B/2303